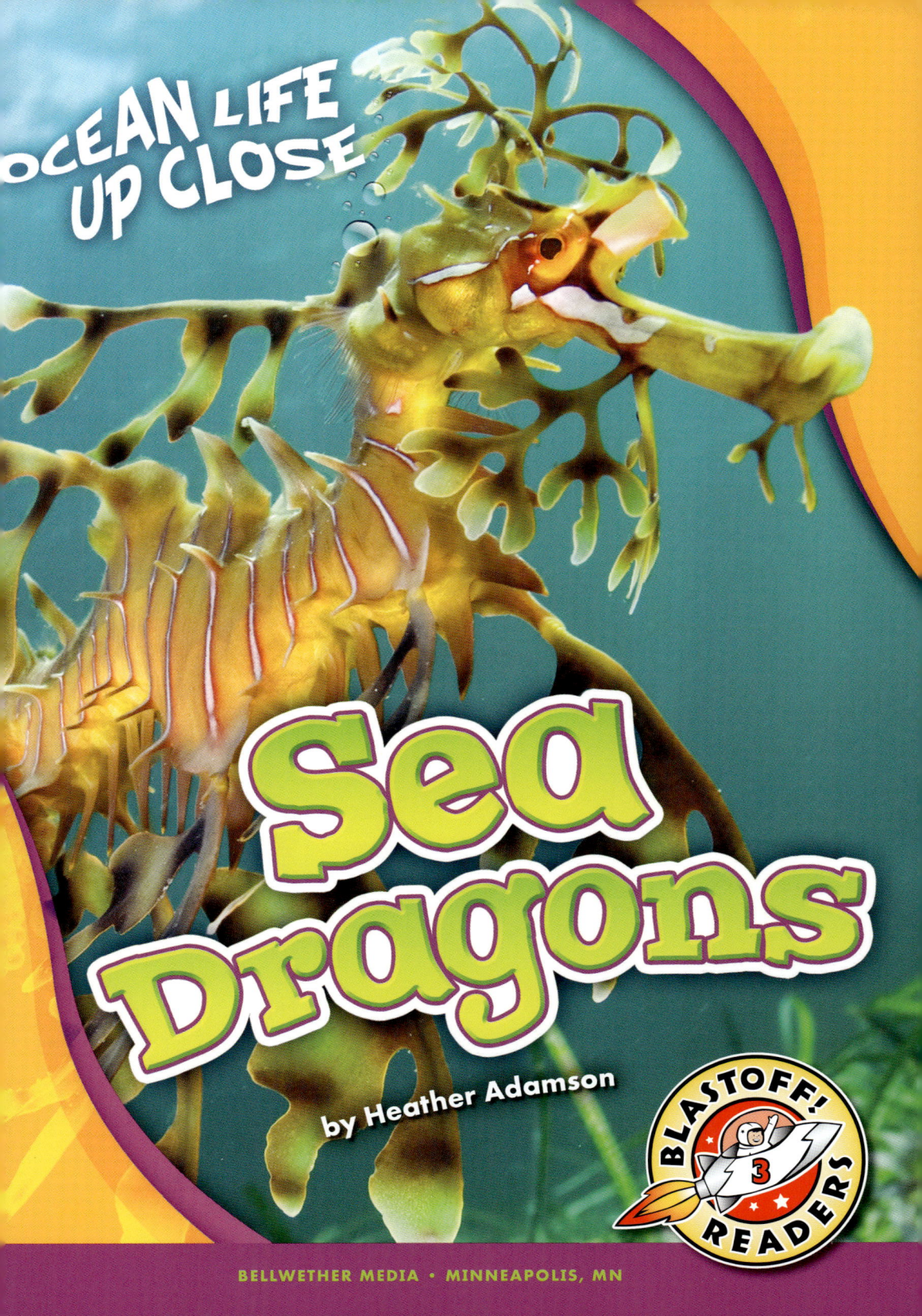

Note to Librarians, Teachers, and Parents:

Blastoff! Readers are carefully developed by literacy experts and combine standards-based content with developmentally appropriate text.

Level 1 provides the most support through repetition of high-frequency words, light text, predictable sentence patterns, and strong visual support.

Level 2 offers early readers a bit more challenge through varied simple sentences, increased text load, and less repetition of high-frequency words.

Level 3 advances early-fluent readers toward fluency through increased text and concept load, less reliance on visuals, longer sentences, and more literary language.

Level 4 builds reading stamina by providing more text per page, increased use of punctuation, greater variation in sentence patterns, and increasingly challenging vocabulary.

Level 5 encourages children to move from "learning to read" to "reading to learn" by providing even more text, varied writing styles, and less familiar topics.

Whichever book is right for your reader, Blastoff! Readers are the perfect books to build confidence and encourage a love of reading that will last a lifetime!

This edition first published in 2018 by Bellwether Media, Inc.

No part of this publication may be reproduced in whole or in part without written permission of the publisher. For information regarding permission, write to Bellwether Media, Inc., Attention: Permissions Department, 5357 Penn Avenue South, Minneapolis, MN 55419.

Library of Congress Cataloging-in-Publication Data
Names: Adamson, Heather, 1974- author.
Title: Sea Dragons / by Heather Adamson.
Description: Minneapolis, MN : Bellwether Media, Inc., [2018] | Series: Blastoff! Readers. Ocean Life Up Close | Audience: Ages 5-8. | Audience: K to grade 3. | Includes bibliographical references and index.
Identifiers: LCCN 2016054957 (print) | LCCN 2017019432 (ebook) | ISBN 9781626176447 (hardcover : alk. paper) | ISBN 9781681033747 (ebook)
Subjects: LCSH: Seadragons–Juvenile literature.
Classification: LCC QL638.S9 (ebook) | LCC QL638.S9 A33 2018 (print) | DDC 597.679–dc23
LC record available at https://lccn.loc.gov/2016054957

Text copyright © 2018 by Bellwether Media, Inc. BLASTOFF! READERS and associated logos are trademarks and/or registered trademarks of Bellwether Media, Inc. SCHOLASTIC, CHILDREN'S PRESS, and associated logos are trademarks and/or registered trademarks of Scholastic Inc., 557 Broadway, New York, NY 10012.

Editor: Christina Leighton   Designer: Lois Stanfield

Printed in the United States of America, North Mankato, MN.

Table of Contents

What Are Sea Dragons?	4
Leaves and Weeds	10
Hunting and Hiding	14
Ocean Beauties	18
Glossary	22
To Learn More	23
Index	24

What Are Sea Dragons?

Sea dragons are fish that look like ocean plants. They float freely through the water.

leafy
sea dragon

Sea dragons are not fast or dangerous. But they are excellent at hiding.

Sea dragons live near the coast of Australia. Most are found in warm, shallow water.

weedy sea dragon

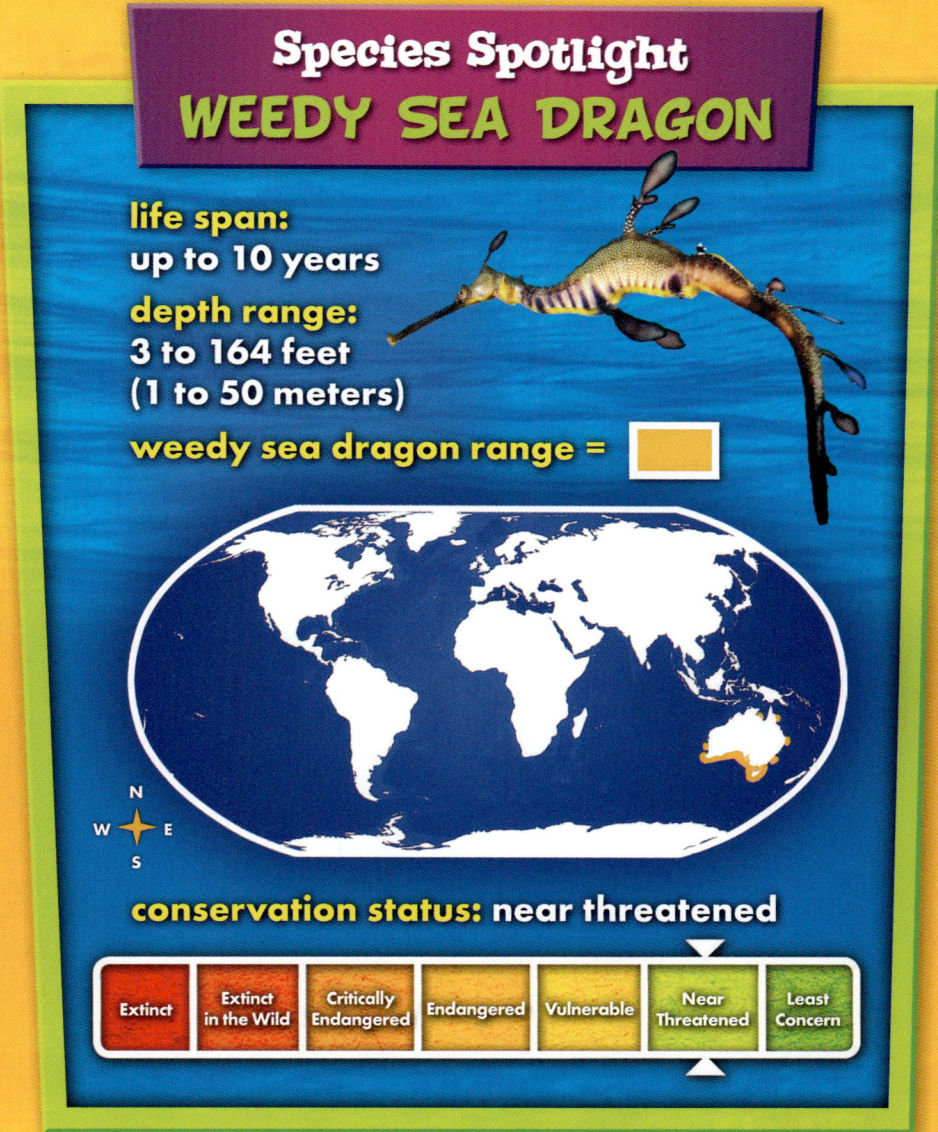

There are three known types of sea dragon. Leafy and weedy sea dragons are the most common. Ruby sea dragons are very **rare**.

Sea dragons are small with thin bodies and long tails.

The largest sea dragons are up to 18 inches (46 centimeters) long. The smallest are about 10 inches (25 centimeters) long.

Sea Dragon Sizes

Smallest
ruby sea dragon

average human

10 inches (25 centimeters) long

Largest
weedy sea dragon

average human

18 inches (46 centimeters) long

Leaves and Weeds

Leafy and weedy sea dragons get their names from **appendages** that look like leaves or weeds. These help them disappear into their surroundings.

Identify a Sea Dragon

long tail • plantlike appendages • long snout

Leafy sea dragons have flowing appendages, but weedy sea dragons have simpler ones.

Sea dragons have small fins. They are not good swimmers. Instead, they drift slowly through the water.

fin

Bony plates help protect sea dragons' bodies. Some plates have sharp **spines**.

Hunting and Hiding

Sea dragons do not have stomachs or teeth! Because of this, they have to eat all the time.

These **carnivores** suck tiny animals like **zooplankton** into their long **snouts**. Then they swallow the **prey** whole.

Catch of the Day

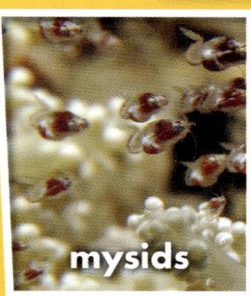
mysids

sea lice

zooplankton

Sea dragons are very hard to spot. Few creatures are better at **camouflage**.

They come in many colors. Some can even change their colors. Sea dragons hide so well that they have very few **predators**.

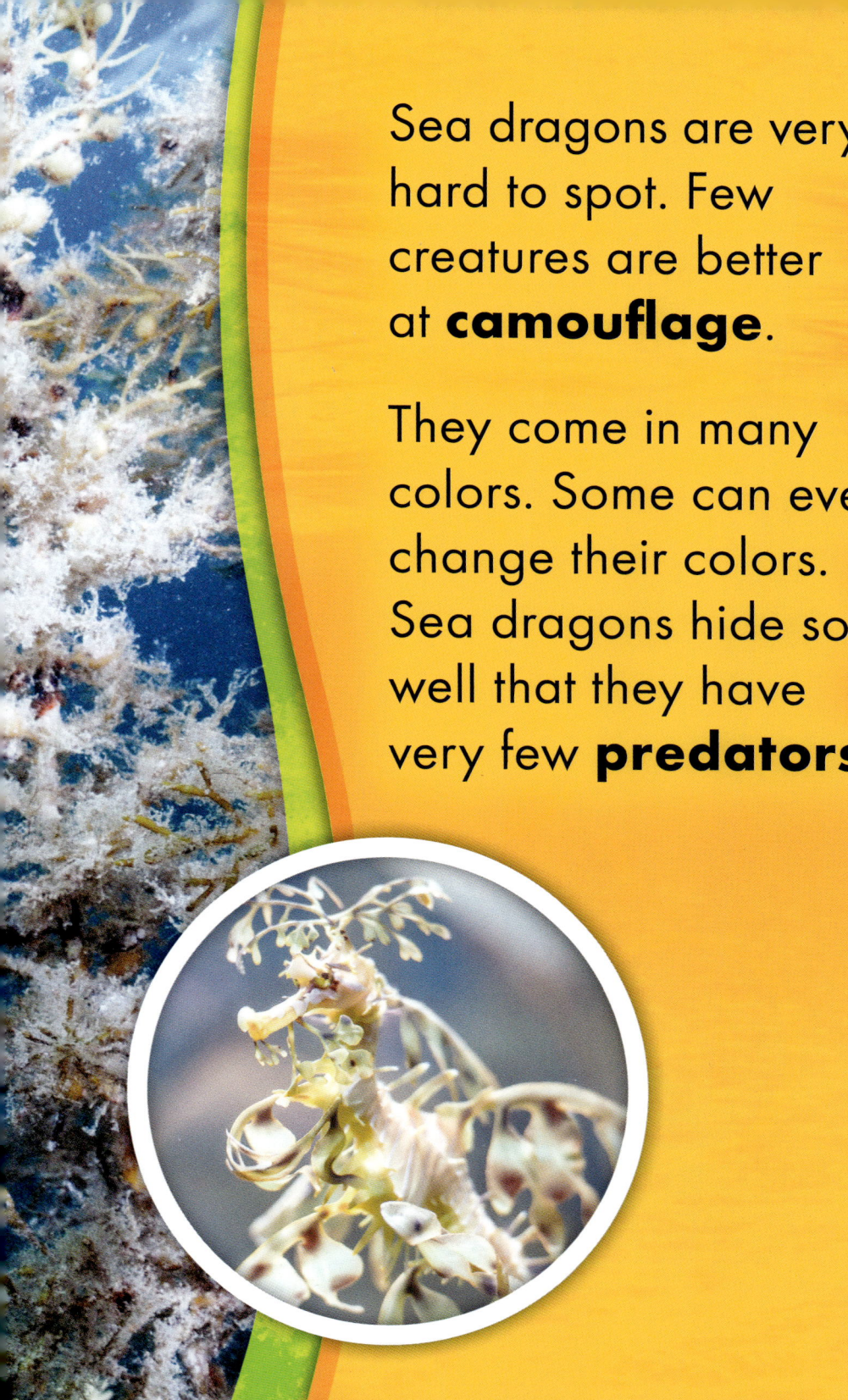

Ocean Beauties

Sea dragons usually live alone. When it is time to have young, females lay their eggs on the males.

Life Cycle of a Sea Dragon

The males carry hundreds of eggs on their tails. About eight weeks later, **fry** will **hatch**.

The tiny fry live on their own. They settle into the plants and spend their days drifting and eating.

fry

In about two years, fry become adult sea dragons. They are unusual ocean beauties!

Glossary

appendages—parts attached to the main section of an animal's body; sea dragon appendages are used for camouflage.

camouflage—a way of using color to blend in with surroundings

carnivores—animals that only eat meat

fry—baby sea dragons

hatch—to break out of an egg

predators—animals that hunt other animals for food

prey—animals that are hunted by other animals for food

rare—not common

snouts—the long noses and mouths of some animals

spines—sharp body parts on the plates of some sea dragons

zooplankton—ocean animals that drift in water; most zooplankton are tiny.

To Learn More

AT THE LIBRARY
Bredeson, Carmen. *Leafy Sea Dragons and Other Weird Sea Creatures*. Berkeley Heights, N.J.: Enslow Pub., 2010.

Leaf, Christina. *Sea Horses*. Minneapolis, Minn.: Bellwether Media, 2017.

Rake, Jody S. *Sea Dragons*. North Mankato, Minn.: Capstone Press, 2017.

ON THE WEB
Learning more about sea dragons is as easy as 1, 2, 3.

1. Go to www.factsurfer.com.

2. Enter "sea dragons" into the search box.

3. Click the "Surf" button and you will see a list of related web sites.

With factsurfer.com, finding more information is just a click away.

Index

adults, 18, 21
appendages, 10, 11
Australia, 6
bodies, 8, 13
camouflage, 17
carnivores, 14
colors, 17
depth, 7
disappear, 10
drift, 12, 20
eggs, 18, 19
females, 18
fins, 12
float, 4
fry, 18, 19, 20, 21
hatch, 19
hiding, 5, 10, 17
life cycle, 18
life span, 7
males, 18, 19

plates, 13
predators, 17
prey, 14, 15
range, 6, 7
size, 8, 9, 20
snouts, 10, 14
spines, 13
status, 7
tails, 8, 10, 19
types, 7

The images in this book are reproduced through the courtesy of: NaturePL/ SuperStock, front cover; EpochCatcher, pp. 2-3 (background), 22-24; Pere Soler/ Getty Images, pp. 3 (sea dragon), 10 (top left, bottom); 11 (inset); Becky Webb/ Alamy, pp. 4-5; Heidi's Pics, p. 6; Ashley Missen/ Alamy, pp. 7, 8-9, 10 (top middle), 14-15; Greg Rouse/ Scripps Oceanography, p. 8 (inset sea dragon); Jolanta Wojcicka, p. 8 (inset background); aaltair, p. 10 (top right); Alberto Nieves, pp. 11, 18 (bottom left); Kevin Ouellette, pp. 12, 17; Jeff Wildermuth/ Getty Images, pp. 13, 16-17; Laura Dinraths, p. 15 (left); Rattiya Thongdumhyu, p. 15 (right); Robin Lund/ Alamy, p. 15 (center); Rudie Kuiter/ Oceanwide Images, pp. 18 (top, bottom right), 19 (inset), 20; Fabien Michenet/ Biosphoto, p. 19; Matthew Oldfield Underwater Photography/ Alamy, p. 21.